Pandora's Box

by Nina Freedlander Gibans

Pandora's Box

by Nina Freedlander Gibans

Copyright © 2022

Cover Design by Jared Bendis

ISBN — 9781626132559

Library of Congress Control Number - 2022942576

Published by ATBOSH Media ltd.

Cleveland, Ohio, USA

http://www.atbosh.com

Pandora's Box - Table of Contents

On the Wings of Memory:
Gathering the Judson Years 6

The Dedication 8

a note from a special friend 9

Who We Are Where We Live 10

The Wonderland of Judson Park 13

Rosepetals - towards memory... 16
- Foreword: Some context...
- April 2, 2018
- April 4, 2018
- April 5, 2018
- April 6, 2018
- April 7, 2018
- April 8, 2018
- April 9, 2018
- April 10, 2018
- April 11, 2018
- April 12, 2018
- April 13, 2018
- April 14, 2018
- April 15, 2018
- April 16, 2018
- April 17, 2018
- April 18, 2018
- April 19, 2018
- April 20, 2018
- April 21, 2018
- April 22, 2018
- April 23, 2018
- April 24, 2018
- April 25, 2018
- April 26, 2018
- April 27, 2018
- April 28, 2018
- April 29, 2018
- April 30, 2018
- April 31, 2018
- What Am I Doing Here?

Our Sun - To Bethie 53
- The Sunlight Tinkers with The Day
- Oregon Truck
- Salve for your pain
- Mastering One's Soul
- Frontiers of Self
- I once thought new winds
- Digging Down Deep
- Butterflies
- Nature
- "A Song in Your Heart no Matter the Weather"
- Daily I learn about death
- Jim Gibans' Mother's – Butterscotch Cookies
- Beth's Masterpiece

Reimagined pursuits through the time of COVID-19 71

Life in Isolation 73
- Digging Deep Down
    - Pain
- Music for Many Moods
    - When Glenn Gould Stopped
- Missing My Favorite Muse
    - Orpheus
    - Lot's Wife
- Memories See Friends as Gifts
- Memories, a Reservoir
- Missing Summer

My Responsibility - My Story 92
Cerebral Palsy - My Story 95

Ambassador of Life 99

Festival of Friends 102

Letters 131
Growth 132
Truthsayers 134

Aesthetics for today / Celebrations of people 135

About the Author 138

On the Wings of Memory: Gathering the Judson Years

This group of personal "collectibles" has been communicated by computers, during the years of living at JUDSON PARK, with Jim until his death in 2018. It was special because he had renovated the building and I had his perspective and personal "tours". Many of the Associates knew him; ours was a special launching. Almost immediately, I could get involved in my two areas of specialty—building on my life in the arts I could head the Program and Art committees, and work with my new friend Helen Zakin and so many others to develop, with staff, a very vigorous program. I would call old colleagues and friends and ask them to tell their stories. This activity stopped abruptly in 2020 when life changed dramatically. The Ambler Court residents, like us, were not allowed to go anywhere off the floor. All public programming was on hold. Our "jobs" were in hiatus. The last art project of which I was very proud was a splendid art and poetry exhibition "The Garden of Old Age" which hung on the George Streeter walls during much of 2020 was shown in 2022 at the Nature Center of Shaker Lakes. This is such an honor. Thus Helen, a voracious reader retired to her newspapers and books, plant care, and we spent a lot of time sharing ideas, reading materials, and communicating with our neighbors on this floor. My telephone and computer became my allies for communicating—skill-building while learning by ZOOM. A poetry discussion class once a week, 3-months of a poem a day (90 poems) and special poetry workshop with the writers of Tupelo Press and participation in city wide projects such as advising on a special Cultural Gardens project. I shared movies, musical events, and many programs with anyone on the floor. It has been a rich life in what could be misery. Life is getting back to rather normal feel as I have worked with Helen and her sister to develop an exhibit of her murdered artists' brothers' work. The project pulls us back to our interests in sharing art with the Judson community.

The work in this collection was done while living at JUDSON

The Dedication

To those in the medical and sustaining professions, friends and colleagues, wherever they are, past and present

Daily visitors, supporters from JUDSON

Special Visitors — canine visitors

Helen Zakin, special friend

Family: Wendy Fishman in Cleveland and those spread throughout the country who come as often as possible and communicate often on Zoom

Jared Bendis, publisher and friend, for sanity

The world's new technology that makes life "work"

"…….a lifetime spent cultivating wonderful things like art and poetry and literature and music and a multitude of family and friends not only gives us a lifetime of ever-deepening joy but also prepares us for times like these when we have to rely in significant measure on our own resources and the passions we have deepened over the years?"

(a note from a special friend)

Who We Are Where We Live

Shaker Square/ Buckeye area

Brick by brick, store by store, story by story. Lucky me. I've been "engaged" to the square since childhood through food, filmmaking, interviewing and programming. Is it best for an evening walk with the couples, the dog walkers, the skateboarders or memories of Arabica's for coffee and conversation, Tassi's and Shaker Square Beverage for special food and wine, Anna Polshek for grown-up dresses or children's clothes at Helen Hale? Is it best to remember one of the first tent art shows in town. As a 'kid" I went bowling, stopped at Miller Drugs for ice cream, experienced my first solo rapid rides to downtown.

And mid-life I helped organize and advocate for the repairs of a crumbling past to the future and present we know. My children were among the last to choose a toy at Clark's Restaurant, pick up an afternoon pastry at Hough Bakery or shop at the music store. I have been a Friend of Shaker Square since its inception. The children have gone on to live in four different states, missing the community connectiveness of the

Saturday mornings at the loyal gatherings at the food stalls of the North Union Farmer's Market and the social consciousness of the owners of Edwin's. These are heartfelt and unique.

The glamour and romanticism of Balaton's at their original spot on Buckeye with violins playing at the table to dinner at the restaurant the night my first book was accepted for publication by Praeger Press. The telephone operator armed with the old-fashioned plug-in system at Moreland Cts. was the queen of information in touch with her building residents on the affairs of the square regarding their personal needs – heat—when to turn on and off – and deliveries from the drug store, cleaners, and grocers. Those seem like ancient history when elegance reigned and city leaders lived at the square to escape the soot of the town and the advantage of the rapid transit.

As Shaker Square began to believe in its importance as a portal to the eastern suburbs, to the national model of integration of Shaker Hts., and its wonderful core location and city population mix, it changed its services: DAVE's grocery store, foods ranging from popcorn to many fine restaurants –ethnic, delis, and serious French cooking. It started to embrace the contingent location of Larchmere full of boutiques, good food and where the major bookstore finally rested.

Fun stories abound. People meeting their boy and girl friends there, women going into labor at the movie theatre, and families sitting on the lawn for band concerts. One time, when interviewing residents or visitors, an older resident insisted that she shopped at HMO Schwartz (FAO Schwartz) and a man said he was the "mayor" of Shaker Square.

I lived on the eastern edge of the square in Shaker Towers condominium for 31 years. While living on Warrington at Onaway Rds., prior to that for over 20 years, our family lived through the process of integrating Shaker Heights – they went to both Onaway and Moreland Schools which gave us insight and perspective on what all of this meant. Current national exhibitions at the NY Public Library and stories in major newspapers like the NY Times verify this as still a national model. This only laid the groundwork for a lifelong attitude.

Later, as empty-nesters we chose to live on the 11th floor of the tallest building on the east side. We could look at the lake, see the storms come in and out, pretend we were in Central Park because of all of the greenery and continue our belief in the square as a haven for the city's populations. Shaker Towers was constructed in 1948 to allow populations that had not been allowed at Moreland Courts under the covenants of the Van Sweringens to live at the square in suites as spacious as those at the courts. All of this is true history and to present generations seems a made-up fairy tale. Thus our neighbors were Rabbi Lelyveld, Zelma George, Carl Stokes, Dorothy Fuldheim, who broke the barriers. The population mix has remained to this day and as other properties followed national regulations the building stands tall in social leadership, a characteristic of Shaker Square.

From a competition sponsored by LIT and read the Loganberry Books in conjunction with the Ohio Humanities Council.

The Wonderland of Judson Park

A neighborhood can be a wonderland. Ambler Heights the place that enfolds Judson Park is just that. My parents brought me home from Mt. Sinai Hospital to their apartment at Cedar Glen, the brick high-rise across Ambleside Drive. So personally I have come full circle.

But the Ambler Heights green starting with our circular drive in front is our own private wonderland. Haven't those of us who have walked wondered how it developed? For me, it has remained almost the same since my childhood. I wondered about its history.

The Cleveland Heights website tells us that "The Ambler Heights Historic District is an early twentieth century suburban residential development of approximately 73 acres, platted in its current form in 1900. Development began about 1903 and was largely completed by 1927. It is an example of the successful marketing of "garden city" living to the wealthy during the first stage of suburbanization of Cleveland."

Sixty-six of the original, single-family, architect-designed private homes, and the JUDSON MANSION, an original home which has been converted to use by the retirement community, have experienced relatively little alteration or sensitive renovation since their construction, preserving a District integrity in terms of: "feeling," materials and workmanship. Only recently have the new owners designed modern homes and in one case demolished the original home and replaced it with a mansion with swimming pool. One Judson walking group established themselves as self-appointed supervisors to this elaborate project chatting with contractors as it grew. They were blessed with an invitation to visit finding the preserved woodworks, gold ornamentation, flooring materials a joy after worrying that everything from the old place had been destroyed. Another very modern home of one of the city's most ergonomic and totally energy efficient buildings in the city. It is owned by a major medical specialist and his award-winning photographer artist wife. None of the renovations were easy in terms of old timers ready for new building types, and the dirt that accompanies any building project especially one that might change the neighborhood's "look." The group which includes some former Cleveland Heights or neighborhood homeowners who have moved "across the street" to take advantage JUDSON's services as they have aged, fill the air with anecdotes from the past. The walking group has visited some of the other buildings under current renovation and some of the special gardens and landscape designs. Residents from the beginning have included college presidents, business leaders, academics, professionals of many different types and architects who found this area their personal dream come true. Their modern designs have deviated from the formal period revival styles such as Colonial Revival and Tudor Revival, which form the basic design look but seem to simply add a quality diversity to the evolution of this Cleveland Heights area.

"The Ambler Heights area is named after Dr. Nathan Hardy Ambler 91824-88), a dentist who amassed considerable wealth during the California Gold Rush and subsequently entered into real estate development in Cleveland. Originally farmland, Ambler Heights began to be developed about 1903 by Dr. Ambler's adopted son, Daniel O. Caswell, and his nephew, William Eglin Ambler. Gracious homes of 2, 2½ and 3 stories, ranging in scale from about 3,000 to more than 8,7000 square feet, were built to the specifications of some Cleveland's leading families and designed by well-known architects of the period."

For those who use Chestnut Hills Drive, Denton Drive, Devonshire Drive, Elandon Drive, Harcourt Drive for their walk among the established tall trees and manicured greens and houses, the challenge of the wondering about the past of specific houses that interest them is ever present. Who owns the homes with the bikes and trikes in front pathways now? Who are the neighbors walking their dogs? And what do the present owners do?

What fun for our elder years to share our special neighborhood experience with visiting friends and relatives? We can wonder at any time of the year.

Rosepetals
towards memory...

Foreword: Some context...

On May 10th 2018, Jim Gibans died.

In April of 2018, when Jim's health started to decline, Nina wrote to him, she wrote him poetry. She wrote him a poem almost every day.

And she read them to him.

Nina is no stranger to poetry, she has been writing all her life.

Jim had written to her as well. For the over 60 years Jim and Nina were together, they spent very little time apart. But when they were apart, Jim wrote to her. At their bedside Nina keeps a box of over 100 letters that Jim wrote to her when he was studying in England in 1954/1955.

She even has the letter that Jim wrote to her father asking for her hand in marriage.

It's a lovely letter. You have to read it for yourself.

When Jim passed away, we were just finishing work on *Celebrating The Soul of Cleveland*, Nina's love letter to her city. And Nina decided to put together this book of poetry in time for Jim's Celebration of Life.

And that is the context.

But wait there's more.

The images of Jim and Nina on the cover are from a work commissioned from Chris Pekoc for their 50th anniversary.

The red sculpture on the front was commissioned from Fred Schmidt in honor of their 45th anniversary and Jim's 70th birthday.

It was Jim's favorite piece.

Every year Jim and Nina would design a holiday card. Jim would draw a picture and Nina would write a poem.

This is their card from 1999:

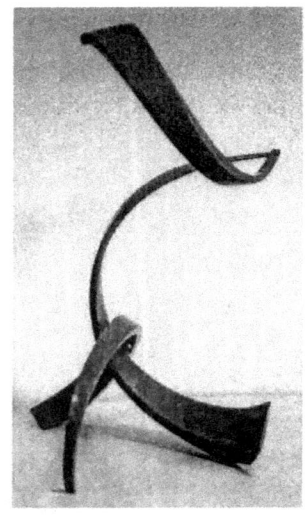

"Sometimes we do not share
dried petals in our scrapbooks;
we dig deeper for times forgotten.
Until we smell gardenias."

From "Stories from the Gardeners"
"18 Gardens and Their Gardeners"
Nina Gibans, 1999

Greetings for a special season
Nina and Jim Gibans
December, 1999

"Dancing to 45/70"
Commissioned for celebrations
Fred Schmidt, 1999

> We crossed America's element,
> impressionistically.
> Changes in a settled place
> seen through twelve blue eyes;
> the second act of a play—
> people in a slightly different setting
> of greater complication.
> We are pioneers in our own way—
> in from the West
> and six years in our own green valley.
> Settled and always moving,
> our friends are with us.
> Hello, 1965
>
> Nina and Jim Gibans
> David, Jonathan, Amy, Elisabeth

There is so much joy in their cards and letters. So many stories, so many memories.

Jared Bendis

james d. gibans

Derby Hall
North Mossley Hill Road
Liverpool 18, England
Tuesday, November 9th, 1954

Dear Dr. Freedlander,

This letter is a most difficult one to write, the more so because you already know what reason lies behind it. But on the other hand, it makes me very happy to be writing this to you. And, I must admit, I find it a bit amusing putting you through the same most unusual situation twice!

You know that Nina and I are very much in love, and wish to become man and wife. Before I left for England, Nina and I had talked over the matter carefully, and had decided to hold off any decision until we had seen each other again after this long period of being apart. But my absence from her has all the more convinced me of my love for her, and she admits of the same feelings. Moreover, external circumstances, as I believe she has explained to you, have entered the scene and have acted as a catalyst to our desire to be married. And I know that even if we had hesitated until July, our feelings would not have changed, and, indeed, shall not change.

To extoll the virtues of your daughter to you would be most superfluous, for you yourself know them as well as,- indeed, better than, I. Let it just be said that in Nina is everything and more that I have ever hoped to have in a wife, that we seem to have so very much in common, and that I love her.

I cannot promise her happiness, but shall do everything in my power to make her happy. I cannot promise her security, but shall do as much as I can to give us a comfortable home, though it may be a number of years before I can begin to acheive that end. There is yet a long ways for me to go before I can feel competent enough, and in fact, be recognized, as any sort of architect, and where this search will lead us I cannot truthfully say. But I think I can promise an interesting search. I cannot promise her a perfect husband, and I know she realizes that already (indeed, she is probably cooking up schemes right now to reform me!), but I shall do all I can to be a good partner. With Army service still ahead of me, we shall have far from an ideal first few years together, but I know that we would rather be together during that time than apart. I fully realize that I can't even say what is to happen to Nina and myself after a honeymoon, which is a very poor way to begin a marriage, but I think we would rather start out that way now than not start out at all.

With all this in mind, I humbly ask for your permission to marry your daughter. Please give us your blessing; have patience with us; and have faith in us. We shall not disappoint you.

Yours most sincerely,

james d. gibans
Derby Hall
North Mossley Hill Road
Liverpool 18, England

Dr. S. O. Freedlander
19201 Van Aken Blvd.
Shaker Heights 22,
Ohio,
U. S. A.

April 2, 2018

For friend Richard

Cranial creases

Beautiful lines

Creative thinking

In oranges, yellows, reds

A little purple.

New forms like old friends

we see and we remember.

grey stone

softened

by years of kindness.

April 4, 2018

If I were not here

I would be there

Where?

Looking at the still frozen lake and wondering about winter/spring

I do that every year

Laughing at myself still warming by the fire before the sun shows its summer face

But it's April.

Which makes it easy to slide back and forth

with procrastination, indecision, and the lazier moods

Like a trombone badly played facing the wind.

I am looking forward—only forward

To twist in the sunlight of better ideas

Because I am not where I want to be.

April 5, 2018

Telling friends of a death

Finishing touches on the portrait

In greys and bursts of color

Likenesses curiously debated as observers,

Confidantes, story-tellers come from the crevices

Each with a piece of the fabric sewing a blanket of truths

corals changing color; crustaceans peeling skins;

fall leaves in VT; quartets of violins, trios

of cellos and pianos; rooms filled with quotes.

we read our friends through the chapters of days

bandage our common disgust with obscenities

by skimming the worst words, not readable for our souls.

April 6, 2018

Rogue life

led by the therapy dog

Wandering the streets and then into our lives.

Licking his wounds and ours

His treats our treat

Patience and a brush of his approval

His tail.

April 7, 2018

Ever since Bachelard dug into my roots

Every room has staged some part of my life

Every day

With patterns for learning

And loving

And hovering and seeking

And believing.

April 8, 2018

Shades and shadows

wall paintings

On my room

My history

A hand, a head

Hieroglyphic.

April 9, 2018

I never wanted to go that way

I marked my life in space

Lined up questions with answers

Explored ideas reasonably

And steadily.

The roses were many reds —

Matching the dahlias, the lush pinks

Parading across the border cushioning

The rich perfumed soil

Until I brought them inside to garnish tables.

When I served chicken marsala with matching wine.

To hosts of friends for sixty years.

April 10, 2018

I never wanted to go that way

I marked my life with

Delicious days

Groceries a treasure hunt for inspiration

Red raspberries in white Arzberg saucers

Well-tested vinegar and olive oil for delicate greens

Chocolate soufflé light and feathery,

My mother's teaching

Turkey moist to perfection

My mother's teaching

Laughter and fun

My mother's teaching.

April 11, 2018

I never wanted to go that way

Even now I check the blueprints in my mind

Laden with red pen marks for improvement.

Sometimes when I put the pen in my pocket

I leave a stain of honor —don't all architects?

I am always making a list of final checkpoints

Edges of shelves, door jambs. Entryways,

Adjusting mirror, towel dispensers,

Are the lights bright enough?

Do the shades allow enough sun?

I am no longer sure, but the answer is in the looking.

Just keep looking.

April 12, 2018

Recollections in jazz

My head bumps along with melody and syncopation.

Like the lives we lead—stirring hopes

And resolution.

The songs of living

Feet — loaded with life,

Sole to soul.

April 13, 2018

Sitting outside for the first time this Spring

Winter has not quite given in.

Is tepid, testing

validity?

April 14, 2018

I never wanted it to go this way

I believed In myself

And others

Now I am not sure of myself

And others are not sure of me.

The dog still licks my hand

Because he likes treats

Just like me.

Soft voices

Feather touches

Velvet massage

And us.

April 15, 2018

I never wanted to go this way

This is too menacing

for everyone. They knew me as a conqueror

sword in hand, brave and gentle all at once,

Robin Hood was ok, but Monty Python is more my style

I laughed a lot.

April 16, 2018

I never went without my Leica

European splendor

City glories

My children – being themselves

Raising puppies (5 kinds over 15 years), snakes, rabbits

Gerbils, turtles, and a cat.

Pied pipers to the animal world.

Details selected

others put the whole together.

April 17, 2018

Roses from my father

Herbs I can eat

Color for every room

Dig away worries

I cut flowers and share perennials

I take pride

Getting to know people

The sun is warm ideas grow

Tales are wrapped in the cutting shears

This moment belongs to us.

April 18, 2018

I never wanted to go this way

I travel with Handel operas, Dizzy jazz,

Subjecting myself to splendor

Filling my joy

On the way to work.

April 19, 2018

Matching socks set my day forward

On pace

Helps me think of color

Bromide for work

Patterns make sense

Albers every day

Color codes my life.

April 20, 2018

I never wanted to go like this

I was open to options

Reading without interruption

Tuners set for listening, not fixing

Simple food —colorful, well-chosen down the street

From my mushroom friends or Kate's Fish

Or new asparagus

Young corn

Raspberry bread from Michael

Bartering meat with Savory

Years of managing food relationships

My friends in food

But Henry's my flower friend. Shared dahlia bulbs.

April 21, 2018

I never wanted to go this way

never in Spring when the bulbs come up

and surprise me from last Fall

I check out the buds

And design my travel route for beauty

The neighborhood awakens to emergence

With the growers, and the gatherers

Stories.

April 22, 2018

I never wanted to go this way

My day comes in different colors

Yellow stuns my steps on the sidewalks of life

Dashes to lighten trees, separates the branches

With positive upward peaks

Bounces my energy

Through my body light.

April 23, 2018

I never wanted to go this way

Smile upon the famous trip to Shaw

Forgot my passport

A busload of friends vouching for my existence

The border guard threatening

In their "Oh Mr." gruff

Just enough to sound official.

Shaw was always worth it

Buried on the festive flowered street

Criss-crossroad to wineries,

Here's to Shaw, the brilliant troublemaker

Making my time worth the risk.

April 24, 2018

I didn't want to go this way

I always packed carefully,

Fitting not stuffing

Folding not throwing

Planning by the inch.

Ordaining the ins and outs of trip clothing

According to suitcase fit or color.

April 25, 2018

I didn't want to go this way

I'd write my way out if I could

Postmarked yesterday

No one sends mail anymore anyway

And I am not a Facebook guy

And I didn't want to go through another election

So I am leaving now.

April 26, 2018

I didn't want to go this way

I still laugh at architectural jokes

The spoofs on us —how we acted or dressed, or our daily habits;

the ink splotch in the pocket because I forgot the cap was off the pen;

the memory trip of me placed in montages — fantastic array of places that

all architects have memorized all over the world;

Laugh at our 60 year-old Paul McCobb furniture

our red Saarinen chair.

I lived with them happily.

They're me.

April 27, 2018

I never wanted to go this way

Drawing the lines of life

On a gurney

The handwriting was on the wall, on the rails, the ceiling

On the floor. When I fell, I stumbled into the end.

In my pocket is a little piece of paper left over from dinner

Got our names on it and my signature.

April 28, 2018

I never wanted to go this way

By choice we were of that mind;

sorry to disappoint everyone

just let me be myself to the end.

I tried. Did the punch list for our building

the building is very good.

I examined every crease of wood

Every rail, every shelf, doorknob.

I corrected mistakes (in my head of course)

Was going to tell you about them when we met.

Soon.

April 29, 2018

I always wanted to play trills on my piano

Perfectly just like the melodies I hear

Every day. Our being together was a melody

Deep harmonies of living

In the same world and particularly peacefully

While buffering challenges

We both had.

But going my way would have been different

And measured.

April 30, 2018

I never wanted to go that way

Or to climb Mt Everest

Or ski on slippery slopes

Or skim mountain tops in South America.

I just wanted to keep my promises to myself

To come home to love every day.

April 31, 2018

I never wanted to go that way

Music must pave my way

Leave love? Leave my soul in the gardens,

and the sunset tomorrow.

Wondering

Whispering

Withering

What Am I Doing Here?

I never wanted to go this way.

What am I doing lying around

Unsettled

Blind and deaf

On the floor-mattress?

I examined the building in my checklist of today

Looking for best practices as they say

I strode the halls and tested doors while visiting people

Tested door jambs, cupboard shelves, railings

For perfection.

60 years

Blind date pick bonanza

Weedless top soil pick

I was a perfectionist after all (just for myself);

Planting on time,

Roses right red,

Chicken marinade in proper wine

Cooking seriously

Proper knives and forks, dishes

From our honeymoon.

Jim in the garden. Photograph by Michael Loderstedt.

Our Sun
To Bethie

The Sunlight Tinkers with The Day

The sunlight tinkers with the day

Leaf tones, like teabags partially wet

Are neither today or tonight.

Building greys and brown city poles stand sentinel as the last sun glares

into the glass windows that soon will be night black

with time rolling in.

You are not here to agree

I will speak for both of us

Because I have known you so many moments of time like this.

They are gentle and loving, smiling with the sunlit leaf.

Oregon Truck

Oregon truck, what have you got
behind the cab, hiding from my view
across the bridge
around the bend?
Three rivers hugging the earth,
framing crops and the seasons,
river salmon caught upstream
lazy living, fishing on the front porch of a house-
boat catching the early edge of sun, salmon-pink,
reflected in the ripples
running side-by-side with logs and fish,
channeled like swimmers' racing
routes?

Trees' winter pink-bark feathering the fields;
mimosa leaves, squash specialties, earth cupping
seed knoll-high mounds, hay lay anew
waiting for blossoms?
Green sightlines growing
rows against a color field of sky- blues
like paintings fit to the horizon
changing with the season?
Oregon truck, what have you got for me
behind the cab hidden from my view? A
cross the bridge
beyond the bend?

Salve for your pain

There is no pain in peonies, roses, dahlias,

gardenias powerful gems of nature, gardens

    of our souls

Their colors, shapes, smells live within our

bloodstream shunting vulgarities.

                      Salve for your pain

There is no pain in melodies maneuvering their way

Sliding through slow movements, jumping with jazz beats

Marching straight to our hearts, barreling rhythms into our joints

Moving our knees full bend.

                      Salve for your pain

There is no pain in the perfect discourse, dribbling through phrases,

Exploding ideas, finding the ears for listening, the brains for thinking,

Causing excitement, blending and bending minds into action

Positive pensive poised patient passionate.

                      You are salve for our pain

There is no pain in humanity, human struggle for spirit,

Liveliness, life, energy, self-possession, looking into one's possible nature,

Looking into each other's eyes, each other's faults, one's own blemishes

With compassion, grace, dignity, love.

                                      You are salve for our pain.

Mastering One's Soul

Mastering One's Soul is

easiest when

Memories return non sequitur and we spend

time— all the time—sorting them for self-

summaries

that hold us steady moving us onward

peacefully.

Fretful confrontation easiest in dreams

that disappear with daylight

disagree with daylight

disappear into the next night.

Frontiers of Self

On the frontline of self

our one life

saving senses stirring

sensibility

pouring sweet possibility into

our veins and of others the

skein of time

what we see

measuring our own day

each day.

YOU SHARED WITH EVERYONE!

I once thought new winds

Would drive into spring

With the power of hope.

Flowers always help

Perfumes of berry trees

Sweetening our lives

Naturally

scents will last

With you, the sun is always out.

Digging Down Deep

Jim

we dig stories, brought
to this place, laid on our
table here
a scrapbook of leaves and petals, shapes and
colors, page by page.

> Roses from your father, herbs for
> dinner, color for every room
> Dig away worries.

I cut the flowers and share ideas and
perennials; I take pride from you.

> mothers
> lingers in the sweet-peas, roses,
> lilacs; sweet smells like perfume;
> flowers for butterflies and bees.

Each household
cherishing and nurturing fresh food.

    Looks and smells and color;

    Best use of our land because of you.

    Part of a life cycle, I nurse

    plants I inherited;

    because of you adding pesto sauce

    I freeze for the winter.

    My hibiscus comes back each year.

Get to know people, the sun is warm,

ideas grow;

Tales are swapped with the cutting

shears. This moment belongs to all of us.

Wildflowers, sown as recovery;

basil, oregano and tarragon;

gardening natural.

Plant-talk and exchange come easily.

Personal tales hesitate

Just beneath the soil,

Beneath the soil.

        Hostas carry the banner of memory

        to celebrate energy and hope,

        heart and uplift. For everyone.

Giving into Winter

hoping that our one most favored flower will last,

we court reality,

bury obsession, turn

over insecurity

cover attitudes, sensibilities

with love for you.

Butterflies

Butterflies come our way

To give us hope, color our day

As only butterflies can.

I have had discussions with many.

And I am old.

Wings drying in the sun

Lifting at noon

You are a monarch

Splendid color, self-possessed

Aging in the moonlight

Preening in the morning

You have tested your wings.

Fully.

Nature

"Nature is the ultimate judge, jury and executioner. Whatever bias you bring to the table, Nature will decide…".

"A song in your heart no matter the weather"

Similes of faith

Smiles

Weekly blooms

Songs

Pierce the mountain of mourning

Within.

Daily I learn about death

Slow soldering

Sometimes unbearable

Sometimes

instantaneous

Punctuating our hearts

Remembering the spring

times of our life;

it is always

real.

Jim Gibans' Mother's Butterscotch Cookies
Beth's Specialty

Cookies

½ cup butter

1 ½ cups brown sugar, packed 2 eggs

2 ½ cups sifted flour

½ tsp baking powder 1 tsp baking soda

½ tsp salt

1 cup sour cream 1 tsp vanilla

2/3 cups walnuts (optional) Preheat oven to 400.

Cream butter, add sugar gradually and cream thoroughly. Blend in well beaten eggs. Sift flour, baking powder and soda, and salt together. Add to creamed mixture alternately with sour cream. Blend in vanilla and nuts. Chill. Drop by spoonfuls on lightly greased baking sheets. Leave space for spreading. Bake 10-15 minutes until golden. Cool.

Frosting

6 Tbs. butter (or 8 Tbs.)

1 ½ cups confectioner's 'sugar (or 2 cups) 1 tsp vanilla

Melt butter until golden brown. Blend in confectioner's sugar.

Add vanilla. Stir in slowly up to about 4 Tbs. of hot water. Don't add all at once. Just add enough until icing is right consistency to spread smoothly. (Gram used the larger quantities of butter and sugar, but I find that I don't need that much icing).

Frost cooled cookies. Enjoy!

Gram = Sylva Hirsh Gibans, mother of James Gibans

Beth's Masterpiece

Reimagined pursuits through the time of COVID-19

Comments from Judson Park by a variety of Writers

No doubt about it: In ways both large and small, 2020 was a year of challenges. Yet, Judson residents have continued to move forward, whether pursuing their lifelong passions or exploring new dreams. In fact, that might be one of COVID's silver linings: Reimagining our pursuits in the shadow of a pandemic can enhance our sense of engagement.

Poet, curator, educator, director, producer, facilitator, and self-identified cultural consultant, Nina Freedlander Gibans is a member of the Judson community who understands the power of continual reinvention.

Nina's remarkable past achievements have included launching the Cleveland Area Council; launching community projects like ARTS FOCUS, sessions for busy people; partnering with WVIZ to produce and direct videos; spearheading a community-wide effort to link poetry and art; and bringing home the 2009 Martha Joseph Prize, a Cleveland Arts Prize special citation for distinguished service to the arts community.

To date, Nina has published nine books. In 2018, she released "Celebrating the Soul of Cleveland" – part autobiography, part history and part communal reflection on what endears Cleveland to Clevelanders. In 2019, Nina graciously shared her joys, and some inevitable sorrows, in her book of poetry, "In the Garden of Old Age." Featuring more than 50 poems – many written as part of a Tupelo Press project that found her crafting 30 poems in 30 days – the 79-page paperback is filled with personal reflections that mirror Nina's rich life.

The fact that cerebral palsy has been Nina's lifelong companion has never dimmed her resolve. "I really never gave much thought to what I couldn't do," she says from her suite in Judson Park's Ambler Court. "The important thing, I always thought, was to find what you can do – instead of dwelling on what you can't – and make something out of that."

Over the past year, Nina has been using her poetry as an antidote to the loneliness and isolation that COVID can bring. "Seriously, the self-created contact with the outer world and telling of our own stories to interested others here keeps depression at arms' length, literally," she wrote in an issue of "Connections," the Judson Park newsletter.

"Memory is everything at this age," Nina says. "At this point in life, there's not much future thinking. But we all have memories – not just of our work, but of what was important to us, what we think life is all about. To the extent we ignore the importance of memory, we are impoverished. But by sharing those memories, we not only find a way to connect with our peers, we find a source of joy."

Life in Isolation: Digging Deep Down

from Connections: A Publication by and for the members of the Judson Park Community

"---a lifetime spent cultivating wonderful things like art and poetry and literature and music and a multitude of family and friends not only gives us a lifetime of ever-deepening joy but also prepares us for times like these when we have to rely in significant measure on our own resources and the passions we have deepened over the years" (A note from a friend in August)

There may have been more articles and commentaries over the last seven months about the medical life within Judson-type facilities than on many other aspects of the world surrounding the Covid-19 virus. Recent headlines blasted the "epidemic of loneliness." It was Paul Meade, my friend who owns Oscar the aging golden lab who has been itching to get back to his weekly therapy service dog visits, who suggested I dig into my raft of written work and read some of it to everyone. Oscar misses his special dog biscuits because he isn't allowed to come to Judson so I virtually chat with the two of them weekly. One never knows; out of these discussions and the determination of three of us on Ambler Court to read-re-read Ulysses that I found out that Paul is Dublin-Irish and his great-great grandfather was one of the editors of Ulysses. My world is made of just such happenstances. The happenstances in any given day come by e-mail, ZOOM, yes, telephone, computer, and lots of conversation with friends, aides and mostly myself.

Ambler Court residents have not been off this floor since March. If you haven't missed us, you should have. Even our families have made 20-minute appointments to see us on the patio. We are in charge of good weather, so it has worked well—it's been a lovely sunny summer. Many of us have our "jobs"—keeping up with the news—a dismal and difficult affair these days, but it does give people A LOT to talk about (for some part of the day); keeping the lovely patio flourishing with healthy plantings; working with Cathy Bryan, the art savior; and enjoying well-selected movies and games much as we always have.

For me, "digging" ourselves deep down has been therapeutic. Seriously, the self-created contact with the outer world and telling of our own stories to interested others here keeps depression at arm's length literally. Memory is a rich resource.

The stories never end.

So I have been writing every day for most of the past three years; that's different from my life of writing when I was managing another life at schools, with children, my husband Jim and the community. This is me at the computer several hours a day. Me urgent with things that have to be said, me with self-assignments. In my lifetime I have written hundreds of poems—I am sharing, because Paul and Oscar asked me to, the work that has come from life now. I am supported by a raft of wonderful friends who remind me that this is ok. My need (allaying loneliness or depression) is to write, read, listen. That is the life of today in isolation. Memory IS our richest resource. You own yours and are the only one who can share it.

Pain

There is no pain in peonies, roses, dahlias, gardenias

Powerful gems of nature, gardens for our souls

Their colors, shapes, smells live within our bloodstream

Shunting vulgarities.

There is no pain in melodies maneuvering their way

sliding through slow movements, jumping with jazz beats

Marching straight to our hearts, barreling rhythms into our joints

Moving our knees full bend.

There is no pain in the perfect discourse, dribbling through phrases,

Exploding ideas, finding the ears for listening, the brains for thinking,

Causing excitement, blending and bending minds into action

Positive pensive poised patient passionate.

There is no pain in humanity, human struggle for spirit

liveliness, life, energy, self-possession, looking into one's possible nature,

looking into each other's eyes, each other's faults, one's own blemishes

with compassion, grace, dignity, love.

Pain reflects the sadder notes, the wars and battles of self

The molten medium of our worst minds and bodies

The greater disasters of other people's mistakes and misdoings

Misfortunes of place and attitude and choice.

The sands of time like beaches of hope perform those miracles of mind

Hourly shifts of mood and moorings that steady our boat.

Life in Isolation:
Music for Many Moods

from Connections: A Publication by and for the members of the Judson Park Community

As I was listening to a ChamberFest Cleveland quartet play from their vast repertoire three times this week on the stage of the Cleveland Institute of Music's beautiful Mixon Hall (a piece each morning:

Beethoven, Mendelsohn, and Mozart), my thoughts were hardly of the isolation that we have experienced for almost a year in Judson Park Assisted Living. How special—clarity, ambience, and spectacular musicianship close-up. The hall is one of the city's most beautiful, with the huge windows, huge trees, and focus on the performance. In the hall, one MUST listen, grasp every nuance. Unusual, I, an audience of one, could grasp this from far away. The setting for an excellent day!

The experience is quite different from Severance Hall where the largest portion of the audience sits on the main floor and the magnificence of the music enhances the experience of the building. Adella on Zoom brings the orchestra players up front, fingers on instruments up close, a totally different experience. The discussions with soloists and conductors make something usually formal quite informal and engaging. I know why Emanuel Ax and Yo Yo Ma are among the world's most engaging explainers of music as well as players most dearly loved.

Watching an Apollo's Fire performance has no parallel. "Christmas on Sugarloaf Mountain" ignites the whole of us as we are introduced to exciting rhythms, unusual instruments, and timbres we are not used to. The experience up close on Zoom lasts for a long time.

I've been to all such concerts many times, some since childhood. In isolation they become very precious—we take so much of our performing arts for granted. I was IN that audience in the last row at the Cleveland Museum of Art. What an astounding experience to see the performers up close! Les Delices, along with Apollo's Fire has introduced me to old and new music. Only to my ears today, certainly not in its day. Les Delices in a quieter way seems perfectly right for an evening's settling in.

My own explorations have included performances of the Beatles, Frank Zappa, and Bob Dylan— new avenues at my advanced age advocated by family and friends. Pure FUN.

I spent a lifetime advocating the "live experience"—the perfect experience. But if I must be isolated these experiences are memorable. I can watch/hear them at any time and free a possibly restrictive moment. I can listen and think, listen and look, listen and hear the best music possible. I have a personal gratitude for this possibility. Most of these opportunities emanate from our own talent in our own backyard, but many many others exist and bring the world of talent to us. I keep WCLV on 24/7 in addition—helps at any hour.

Solace and peace, excitement and joy are at our fingertips, which allays fears and loneliness.

People ask what I do all day. Now you know—try to keep upbeat at a downbeat time.

When Glenn Gould Stopped

It was when Glenn Gould stopped on an F sharp

in a forever perfect Bach

(except for his singing along)

and asked that the open door be closed

the world stayed inside.

For one unblemished hour

he painted with lavender arpeggios

and magenta chords

threading my thoughts into fabrics

into cohesive ideas.

Concentration has that effect

of winding and unwinding, of fluidity

and neutrality

stopping only when the moment came

to open the door.

Life in Isolation: Missing My Favorite Muse

from Connections: A Publication by and for the members of the Judson Park Community

Orpheus, c. 1903–10. Odilon Redon (French, 1840-1916). Pastel on brown paper; sheet: 68.8 x 56.8 cm (27 1/16 x 22 3/8 in.). The Cleveland Museum of Art, Gift from J. H. Wade 1926.25

Lot's Wife, 1989. Anselm Kiefer (German, 1945-). Oil paint, ash, stucco, chalk, linseed oil, polymer emulsion, salt, and applied elements (copper heating coil), on canvas, attached to lead foil, on plywood panels; framed: 350 x 410 cm (137 13/16 x 161 7/16 in.). The Cleveland Museum of Art, Leonard C. Hanna, Jr. Fund 1990.8 © Anselm Kiefer

There are several pieces at the Cleveland Museum of Art that are deeply imbedded in my artistic life, love life, and teaching. I figure that people who are really passionate about works of art are sustained by them, heartened by them, and can recall them in satisfying detail. People who know me excuse my fervor, though they sometimes question or scratch their heads. But there must be SOMETHING that moves them, makes them recall, think deeply, brings them joy. Sometimes it may be where they were when they encountered it. After all, these are acts of talented people engaged in filtering ideas through their magical and unique powers, transmitting new insights and emotions through combinations of line, space, and design. We are never too old to meet this joy head on.

At the Cleveland Museum of Art, I am always remembering, playing with the reverie of all of it. Almost every gallery has something that sends me through life's cycle of emotion. Sometimes I have written about works which cause new explorations. I have brought friends, family, students to my forum. Let me see what you think. I wrote the poem on the right about one piece in the museum, Anselm Kiefer's monumental painting *Lot's Wife*.

The last time I could actually see Redon's *Orpheus* was five years ago, and before that, too many years during the renovation. Such a delicate mist of beauty. My muse! I have kept it in memory, seen it night and day. I will join him in heaven when I am ready. I have had the heartfelt joy of knowing him. Go see Orpheus this fall and winter for yourself!

Orpheus

Muse, master of glorious color

Through music that can be heard

Through dustings of ochre

And purple. Gather your wits

in the soft bed of flowers

Do not forget to nuzzle

And listen.

Lot's Wife

1.

Crumpled in a fist of fire

the world cries

for what it could possibly have done to itself

to sacrifice its essence.

How did it prepare?

play with fireworks? look through a barrel?

carry a gun? spit out bastard words

into sprawl spilling hate?

Why don't we know so we will always know

so our children will not have to ask?

2.

I am lost in the browned meadow

no marked paths, no marked turns,

houses no one sees were homes

peeling chimneys, faded carpets unused rooms.

best at sunset in the rosy light.

all houses are one house

history splays into dust.

stories wrap around buildings and people.

distant cousins known only by captions

Whose family do I share in my family?

Where are we? By the roadside?

In the rubble? On the field?

3.

This cocoon of dust

for souls

and butterflies next spring

for the cayenne spotted meadow

will grow one red flower for each

to take a long drink into history.

replenish hope

and remember the forgotten.

Life in Isolation: Memories See Friends as Gifts

Memories see friends as gifts

Old conversations packaged,

Redesigned stories

Sitting on the hillside blowing into blades of grass

Between sentences

And laughter.

Memories, a Reservoir

Conversations flow,

Dammed up stories held

in contemplation.

Sitting on the hillside blowing into blades of grass

Between sentences

And laughter.

Life in Isolation: Missing Summer

Surrounded by mothers and grandfathers

we dig stories,

brought to this place,

laid on our table here

a scrapbook of leaves and petals, shapes, and colors,

page by page.

> A gardener in the making.
>
> Meditation.
>
> New flowers in every room
>
> Transforming with great-grandfather's figurine.

Like childhood trading cards, seedlings change hands;

Advice to barter and swap for a better rose;

our own gardener's market for those who commit--

barter and swap.

> Roses from my father, herbs I can eat,
>
> color for every room
>
> Dig away worries. Herbs with flowers discourage pests.

> I cut the flowers and share ideas and perennials;
>
> I take pride.
>
> Growing roses for my mother--
>
> A driveway garden.
>
> Annuals for color, flowers for the house,
>
> Vegetables for neighbors.
>
> I read in the garden.

A hoe changes hands

digs into the past

turns up new history

To be shared.

> My grandmother is in this garden.
>
> She lingers in the sweet-peas, roses, lilacs;
>
> sweet smells like perfume;
>
> flowers for butterflies and bees.

Hear the sound of corn growing

from the deep loam and still days

in another place—now here;

belongings and gathered secrets.

    I nurse

    plants I inherited;

    adding pesto sauce

    I freeze for the winter.

    My hibiscus comes back each year.

Get to know people, the sun is warm,

ideas grow;

Tales are swapped with the cutting shears.

This moment belongs to us.

    Mindlessly pleasing all senses

    I rummage

    gloveless, hands in soil,

    pleasure in solitude

    and whatever catches my eye at the nursery.

Cultures twine on the trellises,

traditions sprout.

Memories picked for the prom

or birthday celebrations

or for one broken vase.

    Five kinds of cucumbers,

    old family recipes in the garden,

    three generations on the vine.

    Those that did, those that taught,

    those listening.

Sometimes we do not share

dried petals in our scrapbooks;

we dig deeper for times forgotten.

Until we smell gardenias.

Plant-talk and exchange

come easily.

Personal tales hesitate

Just beneath the soil,

tentatively.

    Hostas carry the banner

    of memory to celebrate

    energy and hope,

    heart and uplift.

    For everyone.

Giving into Winter

hoping that our one most favored flower

will last, we court reality,

bury obsession,

turn over insecurity

cover attitudes, sensibilities

for this season.

Special reworking of poem from 18 Gardens and their Gardens on the gardens on the roof of the garage at Shaker Towers condominiums.

My Responsibility - My Story

Of my mother who died at 39 I only knew that she taught math in the NY public schools and started the Jewish Vocational Services in Cleveland where she moved when she married my father, a well-established doctor here.

Because I am the oldest person anyone knows living with Cerebral Palsy, I was asked, encouraged by more than one friend, professional colleague to write my own story. I have done that but only "for the record" - not for publication or public attention, the intent they had in mind. The public mood about interesting personal histories has changed my mind? How is it morally right for me to write about myself if I am the only one left.

When one is working basically from memory and a gathering of written and anecdotal documents collected through the years, a lot is missing - many times the small delicious tidbits that spice up stories, and make people human like the splash in the lake just named for my daughter, Beth. Let me tell you about four of seven relatives on my father's side raised by the widowed mother and a sister. Their father in his 20s came from Vilnius with his wife. Eighteen years later, in Wooster, Ohio where the tale tells us that the horse had died, the father of seven children died after having founded a clothing store that his 18-year-old son took on for the next decades. That store became the largest general store without appliances in a city of that size (about 30,000). That uncle knew each customer's name, verified when my children joined him at the city swimming pool he had funded. They visited the swimming pool and watched as he greeted each person as if they were clients at the store asking about their health and family. His younger brother, and later his son, was involved with the store for the next 90 years. All family resources were allocated to the benefit of the city, its developments such as parks and educational institutions.

When that uncle died at 96, his brother dedicated the Wooster Theater to him.

He also saw to it that his siblings could develop careers in education and medicine becoming among those first to go to college where three achieved professional and academic awards. He lived in an enormous house within a five-minute walk to the store which had been a station on the underground railroad and family gathering place on holidays.

Uncle #2 became a chemist and CEO for 40 years for a rubber company known and honored world-wide for inventions of such items as synthetic rubber. The family's neighbors harbored a story about him as a teenager ready to show off his motorcycle. They all gathered to watch while he went around and around too many times, unable to stop. This uncle created a corporate then retirement complex in North Carolina worth family visits. Called Dahliaville, it became famous for its dahlias and experimentation with tobacco.

Number 3 is my aunt, who studied sociology in college and claimed she never married because she raised her brothers (5). She taught high school sociology, traveled all over the world with a famous lunch (just the two of them) with Mahatma Gandhi. I still have coral and jade necklaces she brought back to us. A crowning achievement was that she was the first woman PhD at the New School in New York in 1928. When the family thought she might benefit from being in a nursing home when she was in her 80s, she walked herself back to her apartment.

My father saw after her when she was in Cleveland and he saw to much more.

Cerebral Palsy - My Story.

In 1982, when my best friend, a renowned pediatrician told me that I needed to walk better, I first learned the whole story of my life-long challenge with cerebral palsy. I knew she knew the scoop because our doctor fathers were professional colleagues, and our families were neighbors in the same apartment complex. We were classmates at school and playmates after school for a dozen years.

I knew some basics:

I was a two-pound 28-week twin and survived while my twin died in the first two weeks. My father breathed for me while my lungs mastered their new environment. While his medical friends would say "why try?", he determined that he would do everything he could to see that I lived. I was a feisty kid. I was energetic and persistent and achieved some complex projects. So here I am 90 years old.

In between, I had surgeries as a child to elongate muscles, physical therapies and braces throughout life, using every known pain management strategy to keep me comfortable. My father managed discussions with gym teachers... what they should do and not do. I negotiated with teachers to use typewriters (with three fingers) so I could manage timed tests and essays. He made sure that camp counselors accompanied me up mountains and for difficult maneuvers so I could climb with my campmates. In the early days, people born with CP did not live beyond childhood. Doctors did not treat symptoms because there were no sure improvements and little guidance. Young people did not make it beyond childhood. Every case is different. I have met people who are brilliant but cannot talk or walk.

What is clear is that I was barely aware of my physical problems because my father was determined to use medical terms as he and I talked of medical problems: "born with one side stronger than the other," "worked on small motor difficulties." He encouraged me to do what I could do not emphasizing my physical challenges as problems. While the adults knew what I needed they did not have labels. I was clumsy, and did not excel at sports, but tried them all. I limped but my friends tell me they thought I had polio. One could say I simply accepted life with its physical challenges and focused on the other aspects of growing up.

In the mode of surviving and "flying", developing positive skills in reading and writing, I survived colleges with hilly and craggy terrains, and developed passions in music, art and literature nurtured by my father's enormous collection of books and love of learning. I was lucky that this was the spirit of my upbringing. Along the years, my mother died at 39 when I was a teenager.

My younger sister and I had a double wedding. Jim, my husband, was an architect with his own skills and talents and we were married 63 magical years. He was an only child; we loved his mother and father who were older. Jim and I traveled to Europe on our honeymoon to complete his Fulbright Fellowship. We had 4 children, the first of which was born on New Year's Day at Ft. Leonardwood KS. where we started married life when Jim was drafted. He wrote a letter a day while we were separated. I have treasured those letters that are the subject of a film being created by my publisher.

So, in 1982, when I was visiting my childhood friend, I found the label for my limp, and disabilities, delivered by my friend, the pediatric expert, I had to seriously adjust my thinking. I verified the information and went on with my career in the arts. Teaching, advocating, and employed in my favorite places and "flying" with projects with community significance. Researching and publishing.

My physical abilities have diminished over the years; I now need a wheelchair. Just as catalogues made shopping possible, newer wheelchair designs have made it possible to get around. People are more attuned to disabilities but pain management is an even bigger issue. In an Assisted Living Facility, it is a primary concern of the staff so my focus has shifted. Everyone hurts. The reasons differ. The lucky ones have life mentors, physical specialists, and energy for personal and professional pursuits.

I researched to see what was known about CP in older people. It was obvious that not much is known because people with it are only now reaching the older years

After a lifetime of action, I determined I would write when I could no longer walk. The time has come. I write, read, listen to music, watch movies and report/interact with friends. The best combination of activities for someone with CP in old age. Like my whole life, I try to keep myself occupied with my interests. Every day is a challenge.

One day I received a call from a neurobiologist physician at a nearby hospital who would like to start research on this disease. We've met, and it is for real -

he will receive my body after I die to see what he can see.

For someone not expected to live very long 90 years ago, I've surprised my children and family, and have discussed my desire to donate my body to science with my mentors. While they know of my energy and persistence, they agree with my plans when there are no longer pain management options.

Obviously, my father was the reason I lived. He became a single father. As busy as he was in his professional medical work, he believed in being home for dinner every night with us. He was there for support and good discussion. What people do not know is that he was a Cleveland city tennis champion even though he had a missing fibula, he was honored professionally many times; his most unusual city role was as president of the Cleveland City Club where he was on the board for several years. He is honored there at the annual meetings. He was among those who founded Forest City Hospital staffed by African Americans. He started the Surgical Department at City Hospital (now MetroHealth and was Chief Surgeon at Mt. Sinai Hospital for 20 years. He was known for his bedside manner and when he wrote the legislation for HMOs in OHIO, there was vigorous controversy. He was a good story-teller – a beloved raconteur among his friends, I think he would be pleased for my decision to tell this story.

The family archives are stored at the Western Reserve Historical Society, Case Western Reserve Medical School, Cleveland City Club. and in the Cleveland and Wooster Public Libraries.

Ambassadors of Life

I am an ambassador of life
For more than 90 years

A father that breathed for me
Fought off the naysayers who said, "why try."
Gave me wings to fly
Sprigs of Baby's Breath –delicate white
As the winds would take me
And at the very least
I saw some possibilities

I love the way the monarchs
Find warm places
And spend time growing

I had warm growing places.
(Everyone needs a warm growing place.)

The woods were dense –
schools had to be trained
A three-digit typist
Dropping pencils,
In a warm growing place

Heights were hard
to reach climbing
Real mountains like Mt. Washington
or mountains in the kitchen
Sugar, salt, peanut butter, pans
A stove-top,
A shelf, cookbooks, papers, cans
Doorknobs
Drawer knobs
A warm growing place

Telephones on hold with one good ear
    With friends
    With stores
    With tickets makers
    With appointment makers
    With doctors

Sustaining a life
blossoming
In warm growing places

Reaching out
> Lights -- living rooms
> Shelves – libraries – too high, too low
> Stacks of papers -- everywhere
> Books – straight up. on end, piled

Friends carry books
Picking up loose threads
Placing arms in warm sleeves

Family sustenance
Honey makers ---our hive

> Balance and imbalance
> Leaving life's nests daily
> Grounded

> Dried wings
> Roses
> Love

> the butterflies in warm places
> ambassadors of life.

Dedicated to my father, a renowned surgeon and other physicians, physical and occupational therapists, camp counselors, teachers, aides, and FRIENDS

On the Festival of Friends

May 2022

Friends have made me the person I am. I remember and celebrate them with this section of the book, which was originally going to be a chapbook.

I am guessing that there are not too many people describing life within an Assisted Living facility locked down -no resident travel on and off the floor, and very limited visitation. This meant family living outside the city could not come. It meant that residents of the floor cannot go to the variety of wonderful venues within five minutes away, shop, or take advantage of anything now open in the world out there. The closest worlds stressing others with school aged children or employment issues differ with each family, but we learn about them by "remote" -phone or ZOOM -no hugs or empathy delivered personally. So, what is it like in this neighborhood of people up in years without visiting therapy animals, grandchildren to hug and where food may or may not be a big deal even if it once was?

The luckiest of us still have a clear (mostly) mind with political opinions which make daily news discussable. There are about six on this floor of two dozen who even care and some care but are tired of all the confusion and chaos. Two of us exchange books from our collections or the library. The Art Therapy program is strong and encourages anyone, anyone to explore new-found interests or talents. Another group watches old movies almost all day long. There are games, puzzles and "Happy Hour" for anyone interested. I keep my eyes open for the "neighborhood gossip" since I cannot get to the activities easily. I need assistance and my wheelchairs to go beyond the common eating area.

I feel most fortunate to have decided that when I could not move without help, after a most active 70 years, that I would concentrate on writing. I have been writing since I edited the camp magazine SPLASH in my early teen years. With the assistance of wonderful editors, and all of the present technologies that have increased and improved through the years, I now have a large group of books and films under my belt that have explored art and architecture of this city. This and my career highlights are summarized on my website http//www.ninagibans.com. There are the books, the descriptions, and reviews. Non-fiction, memoir, and poetry. The City, family, poignant moments. At this age memory is the most important subject as it personalizes our lives, our relationships with our extended families and the ever- changing community around us. This section of my poetry "The Festival of Friends" celebrates my life with these people who have provided the pleasures of a full life. They have helped me understand relationships, subjects, environments, humor, and the value of open doors.

Festival of Friends

Places, decanters for the wine of memory

imbibing the past, drink to the future.

                      Call up a moment, an image.

        Talk,   wonder,   reflect.

Feed your soul.

A color   can   k a l e i d o s c o p e,

your mind goes awry

The palate of friendship

savoring a universal language on

      the tongue.   Ice cream moistening a
cone

                Melting the day.

                      A chord in
          repose,

The orchestra signals the

ear, ephemeral note

Holding truth is hard.

Candor reveals our humanity

       In infinite detail
            Roads, crossroads, benches
                  the most insignificant spark
                        conjures a
                  universe

The hide and seek
the vast, limitless space between friends
                      Silent rooms within us

Mysterious shelves of memory
Everything takes shape
      Listen to flowers
           Wearing out their color
           Swinging the past into the future
      Whatever that was or is
Whetting my taste for regeneration.

I could not say goodbye
      I am in their kitchens
      smell their applesauce cooking

                hear their voices clearly
                a mid-western choir of love

Applause

Adeline, Amy, Abby, Ashley, Ann, **Audra**, Agnes, Ann Arnold, Andrew, Al, Alan, Allen, Adele, Alex, Adam, Alyssa. Anne, Alice

       Art a canvas for memory.

       appreciation aesthetics ambition alliances apertures amiability

       attention adept

       avocados apples apricots azaleas

       anemone

       Architecture.

A transforms girls' education. Curriculum, research, Civility, Diversity, Racism from earliest years.

Barbara, **Bill**, Betty, Brian, Blair, Beth, Brad, Beverly, Bob, **Betsy**

    Beethoven's benchmarks.

    beauty books bold bliss birds

    business blessings

    blossoms buttercups begonias

    blueberries blackberries

    bass

    Baroque interlude.

Six Bs

Passions for music.

One saved the NEA when Jesse Helms did not get his way One gave us modern dance, and took us to the Madison homestead. A third gardens gloriously right on the 2ⁿᵈ floor garage roof. Reds are best.

Chris, **Carol**, Cathy, Christopher, Cindy, Cody, Connie

        Choirs.

        character civility challenges

        color

        change curiosity children

        cherries caramels chocolate
        cinnamon chardonnay

        chrysanthemums crocuses

        Cinematheque.

Catalogue of Hugs

everything bothersome

and wholesome

tattered and repaired.

Celebration of something everyday

David, Daniel, Darlyn, Doug, Diana, Dorothy, Dan, Debbie, Donald, **Diane**, **Dick**, Dottie, Don, Dominique, Darlene, Duane

Dance - human restoration.

definition durability

discussions

directions/distractions

deep

delicious darkness

dianthus dahlias dogwood.

daffodils

Duets.

D's free speech is heard all over the world.

Eileen, Ellie, Estelle, Ellen, **Eugenia**, Ebony, Edris, Emma, Eleanor

                Ergonomics.

                environment

                excellence

                elegant energy
                egalitarian

                ebullience

                elderberries edible

              Equality.

E saved a city-wide poetry-art project.

E humanized the country.

Florence, **Flora**, Fran, **Frank**, Franklin, Fadi, Felicia, Felice, **Fred**

                         Friends.

                         faith fortitude feistiness

                         feasting fun

                         films and filming

                         foods French toast, fruits

                         flowers

                         forests in Vermont

                         Flute solos.

F's film-life basks in the uplifting

Farmers' markets

Gladys, George, Greg, Gretchen, Grafton, Gayle, Gary, Gene, Grayson, Geri, Gerda

                        Gratitude.

                        genuine
                        gladness
                        goodness

                        geodynamics

                        grey

                        great reads glass

                        gladiolus
                        geraniums,

                        ginger
                        gingerbread
                        gazpacho

                        Grace.

G changes our environment with community-determined art.

Helen, Hilde, Hunter, Howard, Hilda, **Harry**, Heather, Henry, Harriet, Harvey

>Happiness. heart
>
>health heritage hunger
>
>holistic
>
>handmade
>
>Haydn gentle giant
>
>hotcakes, hamburgers,
>
>Hope.
>
>Hopeful?
>
>What Is hope?

H reads and discusses. She keeps plants and me healthy. Best ally at any age.

H keeps the region's planning on mental.

Hearts one red rose hangs on a grey purse, a gift

Iris, Ilse, Isadore, Ingrid

                        Ideals.

                        idyllic idiosyncratic isolation

                        ideas

                        isotopes

                        images imagery

                        idiocy iconoclastic

                        ice cream icicles ivy iris

                        Inclusion.

I can eat Ice cream without dripping.

Joseph, Jared, **Jeanne**, Jack. **JIM**, Jane, Jessica, John, Jonathan, Jewel, Julie, Joanne, **Joan, Joy,** Jon, **Judy**, Jenifer, Janet, Jeffrey, Jalesha, Jennifer

                                                    jack-o-lanterns

                                                    jacks jump-rope

                                                    juggling

                                                    jewelry, jade

                                                    juice

                                                    Japanese origami.

J's magical 63 years of interaction, love, friendship,

J played the piano by ear for a lifetime. She had our ear.

Kelsey, **Kathleen**, Katrin, Keba, Kathryn, Kendra, Katherine, Kay, Keri, Kirsten, Kristine, Kristina

                                      Kindness.

                                      kaleidoscope

                                      kindred

                                      kitchen

                                      kebobs

                                      kettles

                                      Kittens.

Ks kitchen kettles bubble with sustenance.

Louise, **Loren**, Lisa, Lita, **Lois**, Lenora, Linda, Lee, Lucy, Laura, Leon

                                                     Leadership.

                                                     laughable
                                                     laudable

                                                     lavender lilies
                                                     lilacs

                                                     leaves

                                                     lace

                                                     letters

                                                     luscious
                                                     lollypops

                                                     Land.

L's leads thinking about land use and who we are.

Marie, Mona, Maureen, Maxine, Melanie, Melissa, Marilyn, Marcia, Mimi, **Melvin**, Margaret, **Michelangelo**, Martha

                                  Meticulous.

                                  Mountains

                                  mindful mast, miraculous

                                  massive mission music

                                  mysterious missionary

                                  mint myrtle merlot

                                  Mozart matinee.

M mines the potential of young people mortgaged for a lifetime.

Nona, Nancy, Nadine, Nora, Nicky, **Natalie**, **Naomi**, Neal

                                                                                    Nature.

                                                                                    no

                                                                                                        nurt
                                                                                    ure

                                                                                    nothing

                                                                                    notorious

                                                                                   nasturtium

                                                                                    Nimble.

N earthground ---everyone leans-in.

N the favorite author for many.

Oprah, Oscar, Odell

                      Order.

                      opulence opera

                      Ophelia

                      other words

                      onomatopoeia

                      orchids orchards

                      Orchestras

                      olives olive oil

                      other ways

                      October.

N needed to see an OCTOPUS for her book.
Oscar, the golden lab comes on Sundays

Pat, Philip, Paul, Pandora, Pamela, Paula, Phyllis, Pauline, **Penelope**

>Parks.

>pardonable peaks

>permanence place

>Play

>physical practice

>pomegranates periwinkle petunias peppermint pie

>Passionate.

Plaid kilt for the wedding.

   P a library mentor.

      P's great-great grandfather edited Ulysses.

Quentin,

                                        Questions.

                                        queries
                                        quip

                                        quill

                                        quince

                                        quilts

                                        Quest.

family bedwarmers

blue and white cotton for summer,

velvet scraps sewn 150 years ago

bodyguards for all seasons

Richard, Robert, Ruth, **Reid**, Randall, Robin, Roger, **Rachel**, Ryan, Robyn, Roland, Reid

                                        Resilience.

                                        restoration

                                        recess
                                        rehabilitation

                                        resource

                                        Rockies

                                        roses
                                        ranunculus

                                        Riveting.

R reminds us of the poetry of Abraham Lincoln's 2nd Inaugural Address.

R remembers the attic at the Cleveland Museum of Art

Sabine, Sean, Suzanne, **Samuel**, Sally, Susan,
Storey, Sara, Sam, Sandra, Seema, Sari, Sarah, Shari

                                          Salvation.

                                          stories sensible

                                          seer succulence

                                          salmon sage
                                          salsa

                                          Scrabble

                                          societies

                                          slivers sensitive

                                          simple
                                          sweetness

                                          Sagacity.

S's shelter strength   and sadness

Thomas, Tracy, Terre, Tanya, Ted, Tamara

                                       Traditional text.

                                       thrilling texture

                                       temperamental

                                       Tchaikovsky

                                       temperament

                                       tea treat toast

                                       tentative tissue paper

                                       Topical.

T links families and generations.

Ursala

U for Upbeat.

Vicki, Victoria, **Vilma**, Valerie, Val, Van, Veronica

                                                Victories valid vacuum

                                                Vivaldi's Sonatas

                                                vicissitude vast

                                                values, valuables

                                                Velvet.

V spoke five 5 languages. We spoke two. Death creates life's vacuums.

William, Wally, Wanda, Warren, Ward

                                                  Wisdom.

                                                  washables
                                                  wishes

                                                  wise

                                                  winsome,

Wine. Everyone drinks to the future
They always had spirit!

Xenia, Yolanda, Yvonne, Zara, Zaddiya

                                                           Xylophone

                                                           Zinnias

                                                           Zenith

Zeus. Are we a new mythology?

                                          Mindful people

                                          capture
                                          importance

                                          sew the fabric of
                                          place

Make us see in new ways

Food for the mind

                              Fed us thoughtfully

                              Fed us words gloriously

                              Encouraged us to think

                              Made us appreciate place

The aging importance

Of soul

Actuating cause of life

Seeping into our veins

Making us real,

Making us whole

Each name is special. The fortune of this festival.

*Photographs by Helen Zakin
from the Judson Park area of Cleveland Heights*

Dedicated to friends new and old

The spirit of those remembered and forgotten

With love

Nina

Letters

There is something about opening
an envelope
written in hand
stained with a raindrop
slipped through the door
so the dog will not run out
barking and leaping.

I sit at the table with
familiar handwriting
read what I want to hear
say what I think
to myself, and
put it in my drawer
to season.

I will discover new words
tell you about friends who have missed you
give you that recipe I said I would send
plan as if tomorrow were yesterday
and you lived around the corner.
I will pick up the pieces that made us friends

And dust them off, gently.

Growth

As a very senior person I had to think hard about the given subject "growth." Certainly not eager to grow bigger, taller, or along the usual paths.

Long ago (if I ever did) I gave up the superficial idea of changing in physical ways. I left those ideas to be captured or recaptured if I wanted, in myths, children's books – at any rate, from my long-ago time.

At any time, especially after one has conquered many ideas and maybe personal worlds, growth is an everyday thing, a spiritual thing, a way of embracing the mind, environment, insight, perspective - a look at our inner selves, the who we are. It's an invigorating thing to look at the physical aspects but even more satisfying to find inner satisfaction, peace, resolution, solution, belief in one's own growth no matter the age.

This sense of self must make sense to one's self. We are surrounded by some of the luscious land, most perfect gardens, and greens from lime to glade to assist us in seeing the future and the hope within it. I assure myself that it is all right there – in the lilac bush, the rose leaf, the maple tree. I see growth every season. Lovely and lucky! It is there for all of us.

Will we see migrating birds determined in their destination?

Will they be singing for us? To the future, or sodden?

Will they change direction if there are possibilities of storms?

Are they watching out for our future too?

I am watching carefully

I never used to include this imperative.

Shape-up, the monarchs are fluttering

Our cover

Our growth and their growth

Sharing their sense of destination

I will settle on the colors of the world

Right here, homing in on

My level. I can watch for my solutions.

Lake Erie Ink, Winter 2021

Truthsayers

Selected for the Cleveland Humanities Festival sponsored by the Baker Nord Center for the Humanities at Case Western Reserve University and Cleveland LIT. Visit the Video Links at NinaGibans.com to see a performance of this poem.

Truthsayers are all around us –
Buried in the sentence not said
Swallowing long and hard.
Trying again-
Feeling the moss of Spring
Look down—the grass growing under your feet
Slips a note of hope from last year
From earth to you; be grateful.
Truthsayers shout. Stop.
Listen
The sounds of the city are begging clarity
Framing feelings. Deafeningly.
Where are you?
Can you hear the voices of tires, horns, brakes?
Idle and think.
Look up
Is the sky blue or greys?
Clouds leaking
Sadness?
Sun anywhere?
Truthsayers knead the way you will act tomorrow.
Whisper.
Find the time to act.

Aesthetics for today / Celebrations of people

Throughout the ages and through the sages there are voluminous histories and interpretations of concepts of beauty[1]. Beauty mostly from eye point. Where is the soul?

The butterflies know where the nectar is. You know where the nectar is too. I feel it when I meet people and look into their aging eyes.

Capturing the last remnant of civility, looking around at what been gives praise to the human spirit—blind to disorders the cracks in the sidewalk earth's blemishes YOU are to be celebrated!

---

[1] *Story of Modern Aesthetics* by Paul Guyer, Cambridge University Press 2014. Nina was the last student of Thomas Munro, Professor of Philosophy at Case Western Reserve University. Nina's MA was in Aesthetics and Art History.

Celebrate the bridges we have crossed, gullies leaped over and unattended, the solid landings we have made,

Celebrate the spirit of living, the genius of memory, and speech,

Celebrate friends talking because they care, their stories count,

Celebrate family because they do care and always will,

Celebrate stories that spill into every vacant space, important listening even for those who cannot hear,

Eyes follow the paths, but what is felt is more important,

Celebrate imagination and humor,

Celebrate the minds that go back 30 years, 40 years, 50 years and beyond, far better than today's observations that are misunderstood,

Celebrate our wisdoms as we collect them from home from the street, from writings ...

Celebrate knowledge accumulated over years and years of knowing people, and now, with some time one can listen to hearts in action,

Celebrate longings and satisfactions,

Celebrate smiles-they say more than words,

Celebrate fabrics ---the old woolens, silks and hand-woven knits,

Celebrate the August peaches, full-season's summer, juice drizzles to the soul,

Celebrate lilac and of course roses, all aromatics, smells for the soul all year,

Celebrate favorite tastes---mint jelly and lamb, real bagels, chocolates,

Celebrate the trees in the afternoon sun—their particulars of shape all seasons

Celebrate you.

About the Author

Some more context...

Poetry has been a life venture for Nina.

- At Laurel School. Her first poetry ventures translations from Latin and in English class.

- In the presence of poets her entire life. Including studies with Horace Gregory (Sarah Lawrence College), Louis Zukofsky (San Francisco Poetry Center), Vincent McHugh (San Francisco — Retired chair of Federal Writing Project, NYC), a workshop with Alicia Ostriker, and communication with Naomi Shihab Nye, Robert Pinsky, Alberta Turner. Friend of Richard Howard, Cleveland native Pulitzer Prize MacArthur Award winner — encouraging encounters.

- Read in San Francisco as part of the group working with Vincent McHugh in bars and on the stage as a fore-act to Allen Ginsberg's performance.

- Active with Poet's League of Cleveland.

- Publications: *And So I Must Imagine* (XLibris 2009). Co-editor with Mary Weems and Larry Smith of Cleveland Poetry Scenes: *A Panorama and Anthology* (Bottom Dog Press 2008) Piloted at John Hay High School and Shaker Heights Middle School and Cleveland Public Libraries. *18 Gardens and their Gardeners* with Michael Loderstedt, photographer, 1999 an Ohio Arts Council Art Project Grant.

- Taught creative writing at The Cleveland Museum of Art in East Cleveland arts project.

- Co-Director, *Silver Apples of the Moon* project asking for community response to poetry and art — with Shaker Heights Public Library, Cleveland Public Library, & The Cleveland Museum of Art, & the Cuyahoga County Library. Book edited by Neal Chandler, Cleveland State University.

- Read in museums, bookstores, and libraries in Cleveland.

- Special poetry workshops with the writers and staff of Tupelo Press including Ilya Kaminsky

- Participation in 3 month-long sessions of Tupelo Press 30/30 project with challenge to write a poem a day for each month.

- Review for Tupelo Press of Sean Simon's "Day in a Taxi". 2022

"we are connected underneath the seafloor of our psyches" from *Poetry and Healing: Some Moments of Wholeness* by Alicia Ostriker in the *American Poetry Review*, March/April 2018.

www.ingramcontent.com/pod-product-compliance
Lightning Source LLC
Chambersburg PA
CBHW061800070526
44586CB00023B/2653